THE RESURRECTION

Scripture for Meditation: 8

THE RESURRECTION

Henry Wansbrough OSB

 St Paul Publications

ST PAUL PUBLICATIONS
SLOUGH   SL3 6BT   ENGLAND

Nihil obstat: Gerald E. Roberts, Censor
Imprimatur: + Charles Grant, Bishop of Northampton
31 January 1973

Printed in Great Britain by the Society of St Paul, Slough
SBN 85439 090 1

CONTENTS

ACKNOWLEDGEMENT

The Bible text in this publication is from the Revised Standard Version Bible, Catholic Edition, copyrighted © 1965 and 1966 by the Division of Christian Education of the National Council of the Churches of Christ in the U.S.A., and used by permission.

FOREWORD

The event of the resurrection is not described in scripture; there were no witnesses to it, and it defies description in human terms. The stories about the encounters of the risen Christ with his disciples are also few and for the most part brief. When we meditate on the resurrection it must be chiefly with Paul as our guide; for the saving mystery of the resurrection is the well-spring of all his thought, and affects every aspect of his theology. So in these reflections the gospel accounts are interspersed with passages from the epistles which bring out the importance of the resurrection for Christ himself and for the life of the Christian. Less use is made directly of the Old Testament; for the resurrection, more than any other aspect of Christ's incarnation, transcends the hopes of the Old Testament; it fulfils indeed the Old Testament, but goes beyond the visions of the men of the old law.

The texts themselves, full of joy and confidence, cannot fail to be a source of strength to those who read and meditate them. The commentaries are intended only as a help to the reader to penetrate into their richness a little more fully.

Tabgha, Lake of Galilee
August 1972

1

THE RESURRECTION,
BASIS OF CHRISTIANITY

Acts 9:1-9

But Saul, still breathing threats and murder against the
disciples of the Lord, went to the high priest and asked
him for letters to the synagogues at Damascus, so that
if he found any belonging to the Way, men or women,
he might bring them bound to Jerusalem.

Now as he journeyed he approached Damascus, and
suddenly a light from heaven flashed about him. And he
fell to the ground and heard a voice saying to him, "Saul,
Saul, why do you persecute me?" And he said, "Who
are you Lord?" And he said, "I am Jesus, whom you
are persecuting; but rise and enter the city, and you
will be told what you are to do". The men who were
travelling with him stood speechless, hearing the voice
but seeing no one. Saul arose from the ground; and
when his eyes were opened, he could see nothing; so
they led him by the hand and brought him into
Damascus. And for three days he was without sight, and
neither ate nor drank.

1 Corinthians 15:3-19

For I delivered to you as of first importance what I also
received, that Christ died for our sins in accordance with

the scriptures, that he was buried, that he was raised on the third day in accordance with the scriptures, and that he appeared to Cephas, then to the twelve. Then he appeared to more than five hundred brethren at one time, most of whom are still alive, though some have fallen asleep. Then he appeared to James, then to all the apostles. Last of all, as to one untimely born, he appeared also to me. For I am the least of the apostles, unfit to be called an apostle, because I persecuted the church of God. But by the grace of God I am what I am, and his grace towards me was not in vain. On the contrary, I worked harder than any of them, though it was not I, but the grace of God which is with me. Whether then it was I or they, so we preach and so you believed.

Now if Christ is preached as raised from the dead, how can some of you say that there is no resurrection of the dead? But if there is no resurrection of the dead, then Christ has not been raised; if Christ has not been raised, then our preaching is in vain and your faith is in vain. We are even found to be misrepresenting God, because we testified of God that he raised Christ, whom he did not raise if it is true that the dead are not raised. For if the dead are not raised, then Christ has not been raised. If Christ has not been raised, your faith is futile and you are still in your sins. Then those also who have fallen asleep in Christ have perished. If for this life only we have hoped in Christ, we are of all men most to be pitied.

Reflection

For Paul the experience of the risen Christ was a living reality which stood at the origin of his faith. The Acts of the Apostles gives a dramatic account of this initial experience, showing that it constituted for him a call not only to Christianity but also to his missionary endeavour, and his writings ever after leave no doubt that it is the foundation of all his thinking as a Christian: it crops up again and again in the most diverse contexts, informing his thinking on every topic, from the new relationship it has brought about between man and God and its consequences in how man should live, to the position of the risen Christ as crown of all creation. This one fact is so central that if it were untrue the whole of Christian preaching and the whole of the Christian message would fall to the ground.

Here there are two aspects of the difference made by the resurrection. Without it humanity would still writhe and wallow hopelessly in sin: this is the negative aspect. We usually think of the cross not the resurrection as being the remedy for sin. It may be that Paul is thinking of the whole 'moment' of the cross and resurrection as one event in which the resurrection only shows forth the result of the cross, is a demonstration, so to speak, of the acceptance of Christ's offering by God. But perhaps one should see also here the basic fact about sin, that it is not merely failure on our part, or something that requires punishment, but that its fundamental evil is that we separate ourselves from God and all that he has to offer: the new life of the resurrection, and the joy of it, show that we are now in a state to be open to the lavish gifts of God without impediment. And so the positive aspect is that those who have died have not perished, that death is no longer an ending but a transition. It is this which gives a completely new aspect to all our actions and our whole existence, removing the fear and pointlessness of an existence which is snuffed out like a candle.

But is not Paul a little pessimistic in saying 'if for this life only we have hoped in Christ, we are of all men most to be pitied'? The present relationship with Christ, and the meaning it imparts to life and to the world have surely a value of their own, quite apart from the future.

2

THE EMPTY TOMB

Hosea 6:1-3

"Come, let us return to the Lord;
for he has torn, that he may heal up;
he has stricken, and he will bind us up.
After two days he will revive us;
on the third day he will raise us up,
that we may live before him.
Let us know, let us press on to know the Lord;
his going forth is sure as the dawn;
he will come to us as the showers,
as the spring rains that water the earth."

Mark 16:1-8

And when the sabbath was past, Mary Magdalene, and
Mary the mother of James, and Salome, bought spices,
so that they might go and anoint him. And very early on
the first day of the week they went to the tomb when
the sun had risen. And they were saying to one another,
"Who will roll away the stone for us from the door of
the tomb?" And looking up, they saw that the stone
was rolled back; for it was very large. And entering
the tomb, they saw a young man sitting on the right
side, dressed in a white robe; and they were amazed.

And he said to them, "Do not be amazed; you seek Jesus of Nazareth, who was crucified. He has risen, he is not here; see the place where they laid him. But go, tell his disciples and Peter that he is going before you to Galilee; there you will see him, as he told you." And they went out and fled from the tomb; for trembling and astonishment had come upon them; and they said nothing to any one, for they were afraid.

Reflection

The passage of Hosea was seen from the earliest times of the Church as a prophecy of the resurrection because of its mention of raising by God after three days. A fuller understanding of the Hebrew idiom has shown that this is too literal a view — for the phrase means only 'in a very short time', but the passage nevertheless expresses well the confidence that God will vindicate and rescue his beloved after suffering. This passage may well have gone to forming Jesus' knowledge that God would deliver him, which is expressed in the prophecy of his resurrection referred to by the angel in the gospel passage. It is impossible now to know how detailed was Jesus' foreknowledge of his resurrection; certainly the prophecies given by the gospels are now clearer than his own predictions to the disciples can have been. Neither they nor he were spared the essential human condition of the leap into the darkness in trust in God. He entered upon his passion and death with no reassuring exact blueprint of how it would all end; as we in our death, he could only throw himself on God in confidence in the deliverance that would come.

It is to the fulfilment of this certainty of hope that Mark's sober and austere account of the empty tomb corresponds. There is no obviously supernatural earthquake as in Matthew, nor detailed explanation as in Luke, but simply the overwhelming impression of astonishment and wonder on the part of the women that the unbelievable has happened. The impression is all the stronger if Mark's gospel, as seems most likely originally, simply ended here with the stunned reaction of the women, 'For they were afraid'. The reader is simply left hanging, with the knowledge that the intervention of God in history has reached its climax. Without the precisions of the later gospel writers, the good news is left simply open-ended: the tomb is empty and Jesus, unconfined by the bonds of death, so free of man's ultimate limitations, present in the world and to his followers.

3

PETER AND THE BELOVED DISCIPLE

Song of Songs 3:1-4

Upon my bed by night
  I sought him whom my soul loves;
I sought him, but found him not;
  I called him, but he gave no answer.
"I will rise now and go about the city,
  in the streets and in the squares;
I will seek him whom my soul loves."
  I sought him, but found him not.
The watchmen found me,
  as they went about in the city.
"Have you seen him whom my soul loves?"
Scarcely had I passed them,
  when I found him whom my soul loves.
I held him, and would not let him go. . . .

John 20:1-10

Now on the first day of the week Mary Magdalene came
to the tomb early, while it was still dark, and saw that
the stone had been taken away from the tomb. So she
ran, and went to Simon Peter and the other disciple,
the one whom Jesus loved, and said to them, "They have
taken the Lord out of the tomb, and we do not know

where they have laid him." Peter then came out with the other disciple, and they went toward the tomb. They both ran, but the other disciple outran Peter and reached the tomb first; and stooping to look in, he saw the linen cloths lying there, but he did not go in. Then Simon Peter came, following him, and went into the tomb; he saw the linen cloths lying, and the napkin, which had been on his head, not lying with the linen cloths but rolled up in a place by itself. Then the other disciple, who reached the tomb first, also went in, and he saw and believed; for as yet they did not know the scripture, that he must rise from the dead. Then the disciples went back to their homes.

Reflection

Others arrived first at the sepulchre but their reaction was incomprehension, awe perhaps at the action of God, but not yet understanding or belief. Belief is reserved to the beloved disciple, and this is surely deliberate: it is because he pursues and perseveres with the ardour of love (as the lover in the Song of Songs) that he attains his object. It is an attractive theory that the original story here concerned simply Peter (as in Luke 24:12) who did not understand the significance of the tomb alone, and that the beloved disciple was first mentioned here and in the other two passages — at the last supper and at the foot of the cross — by the writer of John himself. On all these occasions the beloved disciple is a symbolic figure, standing for the disciple who is close to Jesus by reason of his affection. This is not to deny that he is an individual, but only to assert that his chief importance is as standing for any disciple who is joined to Jesus in love. Here especially he shows that faith and understanding of the mysteries of God are not simply intellectual matters, but are also affective: Peter searches and even sees without understanding, but when the disciple of love comes he is led by the same evidence to the intuition of the real significance of the empty tomb. Through his love he has been close to Jesus at the Eucharist, through his love too he has offered himself at the foot of the cross, and now it is through his love that he is the first believer at the resurrection.

John is surely showing that mere rational argument by itself can never lead to faith. A certain willingness to believe was necessary before Jesus would work miracles, a willingness which lies in the affections and disposition; and now there is the contrast in the reaction of the two men to the same evidence, one of whom is attuned to the Lord by the instincts of love. He is drawn to run faster than Peter, and in spite of his respectful waiting, is the quicker to recognize the reality. There is always a puzzle in the fact that one person comes to faith while another is not so drawn; yet the faith is not subjective: it is simply that the one is drawn by the bonds of love and intimacy to outstrip the other. It is by love that we reach true understanding of the mystery of Jesus and of the resurrection.

4

FRESH, UNLEAVENED BREAD

Exodus 13:3-9

Moses said to the people, "Remember this day, in which you came out from Egypt, out of the house of bondage, for by strength of hand the Lord brought you out from this place; no leavened bread shall be eaten. This day you are to go forth, in the month of Abib. And when the Lord brings you into the land of the Canaanites, the Hittites, the Amorites, the Hivites, and the Jebusites, which he swore to your fathers to give you, a land flowing with milk and honey, you shall keep this service in this month. Seven days you shall eat unleavened bread, and on the seventh day there shall be a feast to the Lord. Unleavened bread shall be eaten for seven days; no leavened bread shall be seen with you, and no leaven shall be seen with you in all your territory. And you shall tell your son on that day, 'It is because of what the Lord did for me when I came out of Egypt.' And it shall be to you as a sign on your hand and as a memorial between your eyes, that the law of the Lord may be in your mouth; for with a strong hand the Lord has brought you out of Egypt."

1 Corinthians 5:6-8

Your boasting is not good. Do you not know that a little leaven leavens the whole lump? Cleanse out the old leaven that you may be a new lump, as you really are unleavened. For Christ, our paschal lamb, has been sacrificed. Let us, therefore, celebrate the festival, not with the old leaven, the leaven of malice and evil, but with the unleavened bread of sincerity and truth.

Reflection

The feast of unleavened bread originally centred on the rich symbolism of freshness and purity; for when the new grain started coming in at the harvest they threw out what was old and stale. The new bread, crisp and unadulterated with leaven, which has to be allowed to corrupt as part of its fermentation process, was the symbol of new life, vigour and directness. The feast also became attached to the pasch which comes at about the same time of year (harvest is that much earlier in Palestine), and so to the great deliverance from slavery in Egypt.

So Paul can look at the Christian's conduct in the light of the pasch and feast of unleavened bread. We are freed from the old corruption. The old law did leaven in some way, but it had not the purity and directness of the perfect service of God in Christ; it was also a slavery which tended to weigh down and deflect from purity of worship, its multiplicity of prescriptions distracting from singleness and clarity of purpose.

But, as the necessity of Paul's exhortation itself shows — he is encouraging the Corinthians to purity against the background of a case of sexual immorality — plenty of corruption of the old leaven remains in us; it is a perpetual struggle to cast it out and make room for the pure freshness of unleavened bread. Our old leaven is not cast out as easily as the physical leaven at the feast of unleavened bread. The ideal of the life of the Christian is that it should be a perpetual celebration of the pasch in the sense of the liberty and purity won by the sacrifice of Christ, and so a life lived in gratitude and the knowledge of the resurrection of Christ. This celebration is real only in so far as the knowledge overflows from the mind into its fulfilment in action and becomes a feast of sincerity and truth. These imply not only straightforwardness and absence of subterfuge and self-deception, but fidelity to God, reflecting his fidelity and truth in the fulfilment of his promises.

5

THE MEETING
WITH THE RISEN CHRIST
IN THE GARDEN

John 14:1-2

"Let not your hearts be troubled;
believe in God, believe also in me.
In my Father's house are many rooms;
if it were not so,
would I have told you
that I go to prepare a place for you?"

John 20:11-18

But Mary stood weeping outside the tomb, and as she
wept she stooped to look into the tomb; and she saw two
angels in white, sitting where the body of Jesus had lain,
one at the head and one at the feet. They said to her,
"Woman, why are you weeping?" She said to them,
"Because they have taken away my Lord, and I do not
know where they have laid him." Saying this, she turned
round and saw Jesus standing, but she did not know
that it was Jesus. Jesus said to her, "Woman, why are
you weeping? Whom do you seek?" Supposing him to
be the gardener, she said to him, "Sir, if you have carried

him away, tell me where you have laid him, and I will take him away." Jesus said to her, "Mary". She turned and said to him in Hebrew, "Rabboni!" (which means Teacher). Jesus said to her, "Do not hold me, for I have not yet ascended to the Father; but go to my brethren and say to them, I am ascending to my Father and your Father, to my God and your God." Mary Magdalene went and said to the disciples, "I have seen the Lord"; and she told them that he had said these things to her.

Reflection

Again we have a scene of recognition of the risen Christ through love, and a striking example of how the disciples, even with a woman's instinct, did not at first recognize him. His glorified form was so changed and elevated that it is only by his actions or words, or perhaps only when he wills it, that they recognize him. Man's initiative and powers are ineffective; the revelation has to be offered by Christ and accepted by man if man is truly to recognize Christ. Till Jesus offers himself, he is to Mary no more than the gardener.

The command or warning of the risen Christ to Mary not to cling to him has been given many explanations, of which some are simply silly: his wounds were still sore, or he was naked; but these ideas would not contribute to our knowledge of the good news of Christ. Christ himself gives two explanations. The former brings the resurrection into close association with the ascension, and suggests that one important element in the ascension takes place immediately after the resurrection: it is part of the glorification of Christ that he should immediately be raised to the 'right hand of the Father'; he does not wait forty days in a sort of earthly limbo, but rises directly to the full glory that is his. It is only that for forty days he is present with his disciples before the final parting; he is nevertheless already glorified and reigning. But Jesus also adds the purpose for which he is going. It is not for his own glorification but for ours, since he is ascending to his Father and ours, to his God and ours. By this emphatic expression he underlines the communion between himself and ourselves, and that his resurrection and ascension are also ours. As he says in the passage from the Last Supper, he is going to prepare a place for us; this is by his continuous influence as the risen Lord, no longer confined by physical place and time but exercising his power without limits.

6

DEATH AND LIFE IN CHRIST

1 Corinthians 12:12-13, 27

For just as the body is one and has many members, and all the members of the body, though many, are one body, so it is with Christ. For by one Spirit we were all baptized into one body — Jews or Greeks, slaves or free — and all were made to drink of one Spirit.

Now you are the body of Christ and individually members of it.

Romans 6:2-11

How can we who died to sin still live in it? Do you not know that all of us who have been baptized into Christ Jesus were baptized into his death? We were buried therefore with him by baptism into death, so that as Christ was raised from the dead by the glory of the Father, we too might walk in newness of life.

For if we have been united with him in a death like his, we shall certainly be united with him in a resurrection like his. We know that our old self was crucified with him so that the sinful body might be destroyed, and we might no longer be enslaved to sin. For he who has died is freed from sin. But if we have died with Christ, we believe that we shall also live with him. For we know that Christ being raised from the dead will never die again; death no longer has dominion over him. The death he died he died to sin, once for all, but the life he lives he lives to God. So you also must consider yourselves dead to sin and alive to God in Christ Jesus.

Reflection

By baptism we have taken on Christ and become part of his body. This means not simply that we are physical agents of Christ but that we are in some profound way parts of him, inserted into his personality; for this is what 'body' means to the semitic mind. If we have been taken up into his personality we must have taken on his history as our own; for it is by what a man or a nation goes through that they become what they are. So when we were baptized into Christ we took on his history as our own; we were baptized into his death, went into the tomb with him and joined him in death. Only with us there is a sort of temporary hiatus at this point; for Paul will not go so far as to say that we have already participated in his resurrection. It is sure that we shall do so; for we have been grafted into him as a new sprig into a tree, so that we live with his life (that is what the overtones of the Greek unmistakably show). And of course the life that we share must be that of the risen Christ, which is why we are to live a new life, not merely negatively dead to sin and freed from its bonds, but positively living for Christ with his new freedom.

The time of our putting on Christ's resurrection is obviously a many-sided problem: in one sense the life of Christ is still being formed within us as an embryo (Galatians 4:19), while in his last letters Paul can say that we have already been raised with Christ

(Colossians 2:12) and that this needs only to be made manifest: 'when Christ is revealed — and he is your life — you too will be revealed in all your glory with him' (ibid. 3:4). It is obvious that we have not been transformed physically in the way that Christ was by his resurrection and so the process is not yet complete, and that we still have a struggle to live in the new purity and liberty; but the encouraging basic fact is that fundamentally our life is already the life of the risen Christ.

7

THE ROAD TO EMMAUS

Luke 24:13-53

That very day two of them were going to a village named Emmaus, about seven miles from Jerusalem, and talking with each other about all these things that had happened. While they were talking and discussing together, Jesus himself drew near and went with them. But their eyes were kept from recognizing him. And he said to them, "What is this conversation which you are holding with each other as you walk?" And they stood still, looking sad. Then one of them, named Cleopas, answered him, "Are you the only visitor to Jerusalem who does not know the things that have happened there in these days?" And he said to them, "What things?" And they said to him, "Concerning Jesus of Nazareth, who was a prophet mighty in deed and word before God and all the people, and how our chief priests and rulers delivered him up to be condemned to death, and crucified him. But we had hoped that he was the one to redeem Israel. Yes, and besides all this, it is now the third day since this happened. Moreover, some women of our company amazed us. They were at the tomb early in the morning and did not find his body; and they came back saying that they had even seen a vision of angels, who said that he was alive. Some of those who were with us went to the tomb, and found it just as the women had said;

but him they did not see." And he said to them, "O foolish men, and slow of heart to believe all that the prophets have spoken! Was it not necessary that the Christ should suffer these things and enter into his glory?" And beginning with Moses and all the prophets, he interpreted to them in all the scriptures the things concerning himself.

So they drew near to the village to which they were going. He appeared to be going further, but they constrained him, saying, "Stay with us, for it is towards evening and the day is now far spent." So he went in to stay with them. When he was at table with them, he took the bread and blessed, and broke it, and gave it to them. And their eyes were opened and they recognized him; and he vanished out of their sight. They said to each other, "Did not our hearts burn within us while he talked to us on the road, while he opened to us the scriptures?" And they rose that same hour and returned to Jerusalem; and they found the eleven gathered together and those who were with them, who said, "The Lord has risen indeed, and has appeared to Simon!" Then they told what had happened on the road, and how he was known to them in the breaking of the bread.

As they were saying this, Jesus himself stood among them, and said to them, "Peace to you!" But they were startled and frightened, and supposed that they saw a spirit. And he said them, "Why are you troubled, and why do questionings rise in your hearts? See my hands and my feet, that it is I myself; handle me, and see; for a spirit has not flesh and bones as you see that I have." And when he had said this, he showed them his hands and his feet. And while they still disbelieved for joy, and wondered, he said to them, "Have you anything here to eat?" They gave him a piece of broiled fish, and he took it and ate before them.

Then he said to them, "These are my words which I spoke to you, while I was still with you, that everything written about me in the law of Moses and the prophets and the psalms must be fulfilled." Then he opened their minds to understand the scriptures, and said to them, "Thus it is written, that the Christ should suffer and on the third day rise from the dead, and that repentance and forgiveness of sins should be preached in his name to all nations, beginning from Jerusalem. You are witnesses of these things. And behold, I send the promise of my Father upon you; but stay in the city, until you are clothed with power from on high."

Then he led them out as far as Bethany, and lifting up his hands he blessed them. While he blessed them, he parted from them, and was carried up into heaven. And they worshipped him, and returned to Jerusalem with great joy, and were continually in the temple blessing God.

Reflection

To the early Christians the core of the liturgy was undoubtedly the presence of the risen Lord among them and their company with him in the Eucharist. The idea is carried on from that of the messianic banquet in the Old Testament, the great feast at the end of time when the messiah would gather his chosen ones round him and give them their fill of all good things. We see this in the story of the multiplication of the loaves and fishes, with its heavy eucharistic overtones, where the banquet of the messiah takes place already during Jesus' life. That was only a sort of anticipation, whereas at Emmaus, when Jesus has been already raised from the dead, we are in every sense in the last times. The meal already has the timelessness and finality which is that of the

Eucharist; being the final messianic banquet it elevates the participants to the fullness of communion and sharing with Christ in his glorified state in God.

In writing this story Luke must have had the Eucharist in mind. There is the process of initial blindness to Christ followed by sudden recognition which occurs in so many of the resurrection accounts, and indeed is typical of our relationship to Christ on a much larger scale: in so many individual situations and in life as a whole we are at first obtuse and closed to Christ, realizing his presence only after an unbelievably long time. The recognition on the road to Emmaus, however, follows the unfolding of the liturgy: first Jesus unfolds the sense of the scriptures, showing how they are about himself, and this Christocentric preaching of the scriptures corresponds to the liturgy of the word. This itself is a preparation for the breaking of bread in which the encounter with Jesus takes place: till then they had not recognized him, but it is in this moment that they are brought face to face with him. So the Eucharist is the sphere in which his disciples are to meet and recognize the risen Lord, seeing him for what he is, understanding and experiencing the impact of his resurrection.

8

TRANSFORMATION
IN THE RISEN LORD

John 12:23-26

And Jesus answered them,
"The hour has come for the Son of man to be glorified.
Truly, truly I say to you,
unless a grain of wheat falls into the earth and dies,
it remains alone;
but if it dies,
it bears much fruit.
He who loves his life loses it,
and he who hates his life in this world
will keep it for eternal life.
If anyone serves me,
he must follow me;
and where I am,
there shall my servant be also;
if anyone serves me,
the Father will honour him."

1 Corinthians 15:35-44

But some one will ask, "How are the dead raised? With
what kind of body do they come?" You foolish man!
What you sow does not come to life unless it dies. And

what you sow is not the body which is to be, but a bare kernel, perhaps of wheat or of some other grain. But God gives it a body as he has chosen, and to each kind of seed its own body. For not all flesh is alike, but there is one kind for men, another for animals, another for birds, and another for fish. There are celestial bodies and there are terrestrial bodies; but the glory of the celestial is one, and the glory of the terrestrial is another. There is one glory of the sun, and another glory of the moon, and another glory of the stars; for star differs from star in glory.

So it is with the resurrection of the dead. What is sown is perishable, what is raised is imperishable. It is sown in dishonour, it is raised in glory. It is sown in weakness, it is raised in power. It is sown a physical body, it is raised a spiritual body.

Reflection

We must always be wondering what we shall be like after the resurrection, and Christ's risen body poses some difficult problems: he could enter a place without using normal openings and yet he could eat; he bore the marks of his wounds and yet he was not easily recognizable. It is this same-and-not-the-same quality that Paul tries to bring into focus here; there is continuity and yet difference.

The differences he mentions all spring from the transference into the sphere of the divine. From perishable the body — or personality — has become imperishable; imperishability belongs only to God, and everything else is like a garment that can be changed; so by this quality one is transferred at once into the divine world of the eternal. Sown in dishonour, it is raised in glory, and this again brings it into the divine sphere, for 'glory' sums up the impact of God on men; it evokes the awesome vision of God by Isaiah in the temple, when the foundations shook and the mysterious cloud filled the temple, or — further back — the tremendous appearance of God on Sinai in storm and earthquake. The 'glory' of God sums up his limitless power and unapproachable otherness, precisely what makes him so awe-inspiring. And yet after the resurrection we are to share in that divine quality. A third mark of the risen person is power, the change from weakness to power: this again is characteristic of the divine: all feebleness, inefficiency and indecisiveness is gone with the other physical limitations of this life. But the alteration is summed up by the change from soul to spirit: it is the Spirit of God which is at the core of the risen man, and provides his life principle, not merely the earthy and limited soul of this life.

This, then, is the grounds of our hope, the transformation in which the limitations and frustrations of this life are shed and we share in the exaltation to the divine which even Christ's humanity has already undergone.

9

JESUS IN THE UPPER ROOM

John 14:25-28

"These things I have spoken to you,
while I am still with you.
But the Counsellor,
the Holy Spirit,
whom the Father will send in my name,
he will teach you all things,
and bring to your remembrance all that I have said to you.
Peace I leave with you;
my peace I give to you;
not as the world gives do I give to you.
Let not your hearts be troubled,
neither let them be afraid.
You heard me say to you,
'I go away and I will come to you'.
If you loved me you would have rejoiced,
because I go to the Father;
for the Father is greater than I."

John 20:19-23

On the evening of that day, the first day of the week,
the doors being shut where the disciples were, for fear
of the Jews, Jesus came and stood among them and

said to them, "Peace be with you." When he had said this, he showed them his hands and his side. Then the disciples were glad when they saw the Lord. Jesus said to them again, "Peace be with you. As the Father has sent me, even so I send you."

And when he had said this, he breathed on them, and said to them,

"Receive the Holy Spirit.
If you forgive the sins of any,
they are forgiven;
if you retain the sins of any,
they are retained."

Reflection

The coming of the Spirit upon the Church plays such a crucial role in John's thought that it dominates the discourse of Christ to his apostles after the last supper. And, just as John does not wait forty days to show the glorification of Christ but insists that he ascends to the Father on the very day of Easter, so he also does not wait fifty days till Pentecost but shows that the Spirit is given to the Church immediately by the risen Lord. Both are direct and inescapable consequences of the resurrection. Indeed John has already hinted that the giving of the Spirit is linked to the cross itself; for when Jesus dies he 'breathes forth his Spirit'. There is an urgency for the Church to receive the Spirit which is her life and which will lead her into all truth. Here, then, Jesus sends out his apostles on their mission at the moment when he breathes the Spirit on them; it is then that the Church is, so to speak, officially founded. And the first precision of their mission is one of healing through the Spirit, the forgiveness of sins. Once the Spirit has been received then the work of the Church can begin; the new era has begun when Christ's presence on earth is no longer the material presence of a man confined by space and time, but is the richer, unlimited presence of the Spirit of truth and love, which is also a Spirit of power. It is in virtue of this that the encounter with Christ can still take place in the sacraments or by any other encounter in the Church where he is still present and active by his Spirit.

It is significant that Jesus' first words to his apostles are the greeting 'Peace'. This is more than the Jewish greeting 'Shalom'. It is connected with the gift of the Spirit, and becomes a greeting characteristic of the Christian community, as Jesus' word at the last supper shows. So Paul always wishes his readers 'Peace' in the Lord at the beginning of his letters, and the good news of Christ is the gospel of peace. The clue to this comes in Ephesians: Christ is our peace, reconciling men to God and men with each other, and indeed with themselves. So the greeting of 'Peace' is in every sense the greeting of Christ.

10

A NEW CREATION

Psalm 104:27-31

These all look to thee,
    to give them their food in due season.
When thou givest to them, they gather it up;
    when thou openest thy hand,
        they are filled with good things.
When thou hidest thy face, they are dismayed;
    when thou takest away their breath, they die
    and return to their dust.
When thou sendest forth thy Spirit, they are created;
    and thou renewest the face of the ground.
May the glory of the Lord endure for ever,
    may the Lord rejoice in his works.

2 Corinthians 5:14-18

For the love of Christ controls us, because we are
convinced that one has died for all; therefore all have
died. And he died for all, that those who live might live
no longer for themselves but for him who for their sake
died and was raised.

From now on, therefore, we regard no one from a
human point of view; even though we once regarded
Christ from a human point of view, we regard him thus

no longer. Therefore, if any one is in Christ, he is a new creation; the old has passed away, behold, the new has come. All this is from God, who through Christ reconciled us to himself and gave us the ministry of reconciliation.

Reflection

The Old Testament passage reflects with gay confidence on the absolute creative power of God who maintains the universe with effortless ease and cares individually for each of his creatures; to each of them he gives his spirit and this gives them life, bringing an unfailing succession of fresh life to the world. But with the resurrection of Christ and the giving of his spirit there is a radical break. It is no longer the constant succession of new life in the course of nature, which was the wonder of God's creative power to the Old Testament writer; for the whole of the old order is gone. Similarly the way we know Christ is not that of the old creation, but is in the Spirit.

In this respect Paul's practice is curiously different from that of the later Church which has put so much emphasis on the earthly life of Jesus as a source of inspiration and instruction. So great is his conviction of the presence of Christ now in the Church and of the power and strength which this implies that he betrays little interest in the 'Christ in the flesh'. So convinced is he of the guidance of Christ by the Spirit in the Church that he does not automatically turn for instruction to the teaching given during his earthly life. It is the Christ of today, not the Jesus of Galilee, who is the source of power and wisdom to whom Paul turns.

This is one aspect of the newness of creation of which he speaks. The idea relies on the whole Old Testament tradition that at the last times God would make all things new, with a decisive intervention would introduce a new reign of justice and harmony, a sort of return to the perfection of the garden of Eden. In a way the failure of this renovation or fulfilment of creation to become irrefutably visible in the work of Jesus was one reason why so many refused to accept his teaching and why so much of his teaching on the kingdom is concerned with explaining now such a mighty transforming power can appear to be so insignificant. And most of us Christians retain in fact one foot in either camp: one veers between acceptance of the new creation in Christ as something important and all-embracing, and acting as though nothing much had changed in the structure of the world.

11

THOMAS

John 1:1-14

In the beginning was the Word,
and the Word was with God,
and the Word was God.
He was in the beginning with God;
all things were made through him,
and without him was not anything made that was made.
In him was life,
and the life was the light of men.
The light shines in the darkness,
and the darkness has not overcome it.
There was a man sent from God,
whose name was John.
He came for testimony,
to bear witness to the light,
that all might believe through him.
He was not the light,
but came to bear witness to the light.
The true light
that enlightens every man
was coming into the world.
He was in the world,
and the world was made through him,
yet the world knew him not.

He came to his own home,
and his own people received him not.
But to all who received him,
who believed in his name,
he gave power to become children of God;
who were born,
not of blood nor of the will of the flesh,
nor of the will of man,
but of God.
And the Word became flesh,
and dwelt among us,
full of grace and truth;
we have beheld his glory,
glory as of the only Son from the Father.

John 20:24-29

Now Thomas, one of the twelve, called the Twin, was not with them when Jesus came. So the other disciples told him, "We have seen the Lord." But he said to them, "Unless I see in his hands the print of the nails, and place my finger in the mark of the nails, and place my hand in his side, I will not believe."

Eight days later, his disciples were again in the house, and Thomas was with them. The doors were shut, but Jesus came and stood among them, and said, "Peace be with you." Then he said to Thomas, "Put your finger here, and see my hands; and put out your hand, and place it in my side; do not be faithless, but believing." Thomas answered him, "My Lord and my God!" Jesus said to him, "Have you believed because you have seen me? Blessed are those who have not seen and yet believe."

Reflection

It is no coincidence that Thomas's profession of faith provides the last incident in the original gospel of John (the next chapter being an appendix added by another hand). It is a climax to the gospel in two ways: first, the motif of doubt which has been present in all the resurrection appearances reaches its climax in Thomas's positive refusal to believe, to be then overcome and issue in a clear declaration of belief. Secondly this profession of faith in the divinity of Jesus is the only one in all the gospels: nowhere else does anyone directly recognize that he is God. Only on a couple of other occasions in the whole of the New Testament does even one of the authors declare that Jesus is God. One of these is in the first verse of this gospel, so that the belief in the divinity of Jesus, anchored at beginning and end, stands like an arch over the whole gospel, giving sense and direction to it all.

The reticence of the New Testament writers in this matter of calling Jesus God and indeed their slowness to do so — both clear instances being in John, one of the latest of all the writings — can renew a sense of what we so often forget or take for granted, the staggering claim that is being made in asserting that a man is God. By representing God pictorially as an old man with a beard, or simply in imagination as a person like a human person, we obscure the fact that we are asserting what is all but impossible. But everything we can say about God can be no more than an analogical sketch, and any representation limits and confines God to the point of distortion. When one returns to having the least inkling of God's limitlessness in time, space and power, Thomas's confession becomes again simply staggering, and one can see why the theologians of the first generation of the Church had to go through a long evolution and process of reflection and maturing before they could formulate the quasi-impossible.

The last couplet is also a reassuring conclusion, especially after Thomas's doubt earlier. It looks ahead to the generations of Christians who will not have the chance of seeing before believing, and gives them Thomas's immediate capitulation as a guarantee and an example.

12

THE NAME ABOVE EVERY NAME

Isaiah 45:22-25

"Turn to me and be saved,
    all the ends of the earth!
    For I am God, and there is no other.
By myself I have sworn,
    from my mouth has gone forth in righteousness
    a word that shall not return:
'To me every knee shall bow,
    every tongue shall swear.' "
"Only in the Lord," it shall be said of me,
    "are righteousness and strength;
to him shall come and be ashamed,
    all who were incensed against him.
In the Lord all the offspring of Israel
    shall triumph and glory."

Isaiah 53:10-12

Yet it was the will of the Lord to bruise him;
    he has put him to grief;
when he makes himself an offering for sin,
    he shall see his offering, he shall prolong his days;
the will of the Lord shall prosper in his hand;
    he shall see the fruit of the travail

of his soul and be satisfied;
by his knowledge shall the righteous one, my servant,
    make many to be accounted righteous;
    and he shall bear their iniquities.
Therefore I will divide him a portion with the great,
    and he shall divide the spoil with the strong;
because he poured out his soul to death,
    and was numbered with the transgressors;
yet he bore the sin of many,
    and made intercession for the transgressors.

Philippians 2:5-11

Christ Jesus . . . . . .
though he was in the form of God
did not count equality with God a thing to be grasped,
but emptied himself,
taking the form of a servant,
being born in the likeness of men.
And being found in human form,
he humbled himself,
and became obedient unto death,
even death on a cross.
Therefore God has highly exalted him
and bestowed on him the name which is above every name,
that at the name of Jesus
every knee should bow,
in heaven and on earth and under the earth,
and every tongue confess
that Jesus Christ is Lord,
to the glory of God the Father.

Reflection

By contrast with the previous passage considered, the
hymn of Philippians gives a very primitive view of

Christ; it is probably a hymn sung by the very early community and taken up by Paul. But, even after the full expression of the divinity of Christ, such a formulation of his position as is given here has its own special value, in bringing home the qualities of his humanity which was glorified. Here is the reflection on precisely why he was glorified.

First he is contrasted with Adam: both were made in the image of God, though Christ was a more perfect and fuller exemplar than Adam. But while Adam grasped at the temptation to be 'like God' Christ did exactly the reverse; instead of trying to exalt himself he humbled himself. In this state he fulfilled another great Old Testament figure, that of the Servant of the Lord in Isaiah, the Servant who offers himself for the transgressions of his people, and undergoes suffering and humiliation in order to win them back, to be finally justified and raised up by God with the people whom he has brought back. This mysterious and tragic figure personifies in a way the tragic people of Israel, suffering before God and yet providing the redemption of the whole world: in another way it is only an individual who separates himself from the people and redeems them too who can fulfil all that was written of the Servant. Jesus, in his mission of failure, mockery, humiliation and execution, corresponded totally to this figure, and must have thought of his mission in this way. Here, then, also is expressed the idea of redemptive suffering — Jesus giving himself for our sakes.

In the conclusion too we are deep in the Old Testament, for the terms in which Christ's glorification is described are intended to recall the unparalleled exaltation of God in Isaiah, and thereby imply that Christ too enjoys this position, granted the homage of all creation. This hymn then, describing the work and position of Christ entirely by means of the Old Testament takes us back into the long history of God's love, preparing and guiding his chosen people over so many centuries, and into the tragedy of their eventual rejection of his offer.

13

JESUS ON THE SHORE OF THE LAKE

John 21:1-14

After this Jesus revealed himself again to the disciples by the Sea of Tiberias; and he revealed himself in this way. Simon Peter, Thomas called the Twin, Nathanael of Cana in Galilee, the sons of Zebedee, and two others of his disciples were together. Simon Peter said to them, "I am going fishing." They said to him, "We will go with you." They went out and got into the boat; but that night they caught nothing.

Just as day was breaking, Jesus stood on the beach; yet the disciples did not know that it was Jesus. Jesus said to them, "Children, have you any fish?" They answered him, "No." He said to them, "Cast the net on the right side of the boat, and you will find some." So they cast it, and now they were not able to haul it in, for the quantity of fish. That disciple whom Jesus loved said to Peter, "It is the Lord!" When Simon Peter heard that it was the Lord, he put on his clothes, for he was stripped for work, and sprang into the sea. But the other disciples came in the boat, dragging the net full of fish, for they were not far from the land, but about a hundred yards off.

When they got out on land, they saw a charcoal fire there, with fish lying on it, and bread. Jesus said to them,

"Bring some of the fish that you have just caught." So Simon Peter went aboard and hauled the net ashore, full of large fish, a hundred and fifty-three of them; and although there were so many, the net was not torn. Jesus said to them, "Come and have breakfast." Now none of the disciples dared ask him, "Who are you?" They knew it was the Lord. Jesus came and took the bread and gave it to them, and so with the fish. This was now the third time that Jesus was revealed to the disciples after he was raised from the dead.

Reflection

This scene in the gospel conjures up all the atmosphere of the Holy Land, the more so because it is one of the very rare ones which can be exactly localized, and where the place of its occurrence has remained totally unchanged. The humanity and thoughtfulness of Jesus, even when he is risen and glorified, shows itself; for one is cold and hungry after a night's fishing on the Lake of Galilee, especially early in the year at Eastertime, and a fire and breakfast ready prepared would be a welcoming sight as the boat nears the shore in the grey morning while the sun rises beyond the range of hills to the east of the lake. We can trust the traditional place at the north-west corner of the lake; for there warm springs flow into the water and attract the fish in the early part of the year, as the fishermen from Capernaum, barely a mile away, would certainly know. The shore is low and pebbly, with scrub and a few palm trees, and it is easy to visualize Jesus on the slight promontory beside the warm springs.

The scene is a sort of second conversion; for it is clear that the apostles, led by Peter, were reverting to their old trade in desperation. Again, as at the tomb, it is the disciple whom Jesus loved who first recognizes the truth about the risen Lord, responding with the instincts of love, and providing a model for the response of every future disciple whom Jesus loves. Then finally there is the mysterious recognition and non-recognition: they do not dare to ask 'Who are you?', but the very desire shows that there is something puzzling, although in their heart of hearts they know it is the Lord. The situation is much like that of the Christian recognizing Christ in the circumstances of life: he is there and yet he is absent, or he is there and yet not as one expected; the recognition is not obvious, and it needs the attraction of love to see him there. The apostles have turned away, back to their old activities, but Jesus pursues them, just as God pursued Israel through the Old Testament, and draws them from their everyday life to himself. The meeting is sealed by what is at least reminiscent of the Eucharist, which remains the prime meeting-place of the risen Lord and his disciples.

14

THE FIRST-BORN OF CREATION

Wisdom 7:25—8:1

For she is a breath of the power of God,
and a pure emanation of the glory of the Almighty;
therefore nothing defiled gains entrance into her.
For she is a reflection of eternal light,
a spotless mirror of the working of God,
and an image of his goodness.
Though she is but one, she can do all things,
and while remaining in herself, she renews all things;
in every generation she passes into holy souls
and makes them friends of God, and prophets;
for God loves nothing so much as the man
    who lives with wisdom.
For she is more beautiful than the sun,
and excels every constellation of the stars.
Compared with the light she is found to be superior,
for it is succeeded by the night,
but against wisdom evil does not prevail.
She reaches mightily from one end
of the earth to the other,
and she orders all things well.

Colossians 1:15-20

He is the image of the invisible God,
the first-born of all creation;

for in him all things were created,
in heaven and on earth,
visible and invisible,
whether thrones or dominations
or principalities or authorities —
all things were created through him and for him.
He is before all things,
and in him all things hold together.
He is the head of the body,
the Church.
He is the beginning,
the first-born from the dead,
that in everything he might be pre-eminent.
For in him
all the fullness of God was pleased to dwell,
and through him to reconcile to himself all things,
whether on earth or in heaven,
making peace
by the blood of his cross.

Reflection

In Colossians Paul sets out to show how glorious is
Christ's position in the universe. He is countering those
who claimed that Christ was simply one supernatural
being among many, and in this passage he does it in
two ways. First he takes up the description of the
Wisdom of God in the Old Testament; from these verses
of the Book of Wisdom it is not clear whether Wisdom
is separate from God; it is the power of God at work
in the world, the extension of himself, emanating from
him, yet reflecting him perfectly and remaining his own.
In short it is what makes the inaccessible God close to
us and an active force among us. Paul sees that this is
Christ's position by virtue of his relationship to God;
it is through him that creation comes about, so that

the ultimate ground of creation is in him. Not only that, but all things were created for him; he is the ultimate reason for creation, in that creation finds its finality in him, and he is its principle of unity. The function of Christ in the universe is all-embracing; without him it neither makes sense nor even exists. Directly it is he who is responsible for it and God only through him, so that even in this he is our way to God.

In the same way as he is the principle of creation, so the resurrection makes him the principle of the new life of the resurrection. If he were not, he would fall sadly behind; but as it is he holds the active superiority in every way: the Church is his body and in him is 'the fullness'. This word takes us back into the rich world of oriental myth, the pantheistic idea that the universe is filled by God and fills up God; Paul adopts this idea to express that Christ is all in all: as well as being head in a special way of his body which is the Church, he is the principle of unity and the ground of being for all things. Redeemed creation of which he is the principle does not extend simply to men, but embraces all things, brought into unity and reconciled through and in him. Thus his natural headship of creation receives a new dimension in re-creation.

15

THE PROMISE TO PETER

Matthew 16:16-19

Simon Peter replied, "You are the Christ, the Son of the living God." And Jesus answered him, "Blessed are you, Simon Bar-Jona! For flesh and blood has not revealed this to you, but my Father who is in heaven. And I tell you, you are Peter, and on this rock I will build my church, and the powers of death shall not prevail against it. I will give you the keys of the kingdom of heaven, and whatever you bind on earth shall be bound in heaven, and whatever you loose on earth shall be loosed in heaven."

John 10:1-6, 8, 10-13

"Truly, truly, I say to you, he who does not enter the sheepfold by the door but climbs in by another way, that man is a thief and a robber; but he who enters by the door is the shepherd of the sheep. To him the gatekeeper opens; the sheep hear his voice, and he calls his own sheep by name and leads them out. When he has brought out all his own, he goes before them, and the sheep follow him, for they know his voice. A stranger they will not follow, but they will flee from him, for they do not know the voice of strangers." This figure Jesus used with them, but they did not understand what he was saying to them.

"All who came before me are thieves and robbers; but the sheep did not heed them. The thief comes only to steal and kill and destroy; I came that they may have life, and have it abundantly. I am the good shepherd. The good shepherd lays down his life for the sheep. He who is a hireling and not a shepherd, whose own the sheep are not, sees the wolf coming and leaves the sheep and flees; and the wolf snatches them and scatters them. He flees because he is a hireling and cares nothing for the sheep."

John 21:15-19

When they had finished breakfast, Jesus said to Simon Peter, "Simon, son of John, do you love me more than these?" He said to him, "Yes, Lord; you know that I love you." He said to him, "Feed my lambs." A second time he said to him, "Simon, son of John, do you love me?" He said to him, "Yes, Lord; you know that I love you." He said to him, "Tend my sheep." He said to him the third time, "Simon, son of John, do you love me?" Peter was grieved because he said to him the third time, "Do you love me?" And he said him, "Lord, you know everything; you know that I love you." Jesus said to him, "Feed my sheep. Truly, truly, I say to you, when you were young, you girded yourself and walked where you would; but when you are old, you will stretch out your hands, and another will gird you and carry you where you do not wish to go." (This he said to show by what death he was to glorify God.) And after this he said to him, "Follow me."

Reflection

It is interesting to contrast Jesus' words to Peter here with his words to him at Caesarea Philippi in Matthew's gospel. There Jesus gave a promise of juridical power to the head of his community; here he demands love from the shepherd of the flock and predicts that he will suffer after the model of his master. From this passage and that of the good shepherd we can see that he conceives the function of shepherd in the dual role of love and suffering. Simon must love his master more than the others (and the triple repetition which so upsets Peter, must correspond to the emphatic triple denial in the courtyard of the high priest); unless he does this he cannot take the place of the good shepherd in loving and caring for the flock. Love of the flock must be the expression of love of Christ. This is not to say that the shepherd does not love the sheep for themselves, but a lover sees his beloved in everything connected with the beloved, and thereby genuinely loves them for their own sake, by a sort of superabundant overflow of the joy and warmth of love. Just so the saints genuinely love those whom they serve and for their own sake, because each individual is the image of Christ and is loved by Christ. Without this genuine love of the sheep in Christ but for themselves no true pastoral work can take place. Perhaps the most significant point is that Christ does not ask Peter whether he loves the sheep or wants to be the shepherd; the only question is whether Peter loves Christ, since love of his sheep inevitably follows from love of Christ.

Is it a coincidence that the idea of suffering follows on the promise to Peter both in John and in Matthew? Is it because the pastor must follow Christ as master, and this following Christ must inevitably bring suffering? Or is the connection more immediate, that pastoral care must always bring suffering? Perhaps it is that the sheep are always ungrateful or unresponsive, perhaps that the shepherd must always give himself to the sheep in disregard of his own preferences and comfort.

16

RENEWAL IN CHRIST

2 Corinthians 3:16-18

But when a man turns to the Lord the veil is removed. Now the Lord is the Spirit, and where the Spirit of the Lord is, there is freedom. And we all, with unveiled face, beholding the glory of the Lord, are being changed into his likeness from one degree of glory to another; for this comes from the Lord who is the Spirit.

Colossians 3:1-12

If then you have been raised with Christ, seek the things that are above, where Christ is, seated at the right hand of God. Set your minds on things that are above, not on things that are on earth. For you have died, and your life is hid with Christ in God. When Christ who is our life appears, then you also will appear with him in glory.

Put to death therefore what is earthly in you: immorality, impurity, passion, evil desire, and covetousness, which is idolatry. On account of these the wrath of God is coming. In these you once walked, when you lived in them. But now put them all away: anger, wrath, malice, slander, and foul talk from your mouth. Do not lie to one another, seeing that you have put off the old nature with its practices and have put on the new nature, which is being renewed in knowledge after the image of its creator. Here there cannot be Greek and Jew, circumcised and uncircumcised, barbarian, Scythian, slave, free man, but Christ is all, and in all.

Put on then, as God's chosen ones, holy and beloved, compassion, kindness, lowliness, meekness, and patience.

Reflection

In Colossians, late on in his life, Paul reverts once again to the thought that we live now with Christ's own life; for we have been grafted into him and have taken on, so to speak, his heart-beats, and his history has become our own. We have already been raised up with him, so already share his risen life, though in a hidden way; it has yet to be made manifest. Writing earlier to the Romans Paul had put the same truth, delicately balanced between 'already' and 'not yet', differently, that we had already died with Christ but not yet been raised. Now, perhaps because his hope in an early appearance of Christ to end the world has waned, and he has settled down more to the idea that the Christian must live out his life in the world, he is more optimistic about what has already been achieved: already we live with the full life of the risen Christ, already we are in heaven, but in a hidden fashion: the 'not yet' is confined to the open manifestation of what already is cryptically. The great difference between these two statements at different stages of Paul's development is that now he sees that the natural state for the Christian is that he is, even now, in heaven, in full communication with God and the full joy of his vision and presence, but that temporarily, almost by accident as it were, this does not appear. The natural state is that we should be in full possession of the beatific vision, and our life and pre-occupations those of the saints in heaven; our true self is that new self which is ours in Christ.

And yet, as the verse from Corinthians shows, the process is in a way incomplete. We reflect the image of Christ, the image of the Father which is Christ, who himself reflects and embodies perfectly all that the Father is. We too are to reflect this and become perfect images of Christ — it is another way of expressing our sharing in the life of Christ; for to the ancients the image is another exemplar of the reality, not a substance-less, superficial not an appearance — and yet the process is a long one.

According to both these ways of putting it, the basic transformation of ourselves by Christ's resurrection has already taken place: but Paul's exhortations in Colossians show clearly that he is not blind to the struggle which must still go on to make this a reality for us.

17

'STAY BEHIND UNTIL I COME'

Revelation 1:1-8

John to the seven churches that are in Asia:

Grace to you and peace from him who is and who was and who is to come, and from the seven spirits who are before his throne, and from Jesus Christ the faithful witness, the first-born of the dead, and the ruler of kings on earth.

To him who loves us and has freed us from our sins by his blood and made us a kingdom, priests to his God and Father, to him be glory and dominion for ever and ever. Amen. Behold, he is coming with the clouds, and every eye will see him, every one who pierced him; and all tribes of the earth will wail on account of him. Even so. Amen.

"I am the Alpha and the Omega," says the Lord God, who is and who was and who is to come, the Almighty.

John 21:20-23

Peter turned and saw following them the disciple whom Jesus loved, who had lain close to his breast at the supper and had said, "Lord, who is it that is going to betray you?" When Peter saw him, he said to Jesus, "Lord, what about this man?" Jesus said to him, "If it is my will that he remain until I come, what is that to you? Follow me!" The saying spread abroad among the brethren that this disciple was not to die; yet Jesus did not say to him that he was not to die, but, "If it is my will that he remain until I come, what is that to you?"

Reflection

The last scene of the gospel of John seems to enshrine some old controversy about the death of the beloved disciple, or at least so it has always been interpreted, in the light of the tradition that John lived to a great old age. More important than the actual controversy — which was perhaps about whether Christ had promised that John would never die — is the vivid expectancy of the early Christians that Christ was soon to come. This finds its clearest expression in the book of Revelation, where the expectancy reaches a fever pitch which constitutes it the controlling factor in the whole mentality of the book. On the whole it seems that this expectation that Christ would come again in the immediate future was inherited from the Jewish hopes, according to which the messiah would come as the immediate herald of God's reign on earth, ushering in the final paradisiac state. Since Jesus did not obviously bring this state by his earthly life, a second coming could not be long delayed. It was only as the delay grew longer that reflection showed he had after all already brought this state in a less spectacular form, and that its reality consisted of the presence of the holy Spirit in the faithful and the working of Christ's risen life within them.

Nevertheless the expectation of Christ's second coming still persists: he is still the one 'who is to come' and complete the liberation he has begun. Only this coming to which we look forward is not in the form of cosmic upheaval, and is more an encounter in which we go to meet him. It is the affectionate meeting between the Christ and the beloved disciple in which he fetches the disciple away to be with himself in the fullness of his love, the end of that separation which persists while we still see only 'through a glass darkly'.

18

CHRIST, THE HEAD OF THE BODY

1 Corinthians 12:12-27

For just as the body is one and has many members, and
all the members of the body, though many, are one
body, so it is with Christ. For by one Spirit we were
all baptized into one body — Jews or Greeks, slaves or
free — and all were made to drink of one Spirit.

For the body does not consist of one member but of
many. If the foot should say, "Because I am not a hand,
I do not belong to the body," that would not make it
any less a part of the body. And if the ear should say,
"Because I am not an eye, I do not belong to the body,"
that would not make it any less a part of the body. If
the whole body were an eye, where would be the hearing?
If the whole body were an ear, where would be the sense
of smell? But as it is, God arranged the organs in the
body, each of them, as he chose. If all were a single
organ, where would the body be? As it is, there are
many parts, yet one body. The eye cannot say to the
hand, "I have no need of you," nor again the head to
the feet, "I have no need of you." On the contrary, the
parts of the body which seem to be weaker are indis-
pensable, and those parts of the body which we think
less honourable we invest with the greater honour, and
our unpresentable parts are treated with greater modesty,
which our more presentable parts do not require. But

God has so adjusted the body, giving the greater honour to the inferior part, that there may be no discord in the body, but that the members may have the same care for one another. If one member suffers, all suffer together; if one member is honoured, all rejoice together.

Now you are the body of Christ and individually members of it.

Ephesians 1:16-23

I do not cease to give thanks for you, remembering you in my prayers, that the God of our Lord Jesus Christ, the Father of glory, may give you a spirit of wisdom and of revelation in the knowledge of him, having the eyes of your hearts enlightened, that you may know what is the hope to which he has called you, what are the riches of his glorious inheritance in the saints, and what is the immeasurable greatness of his power in us who believe, according to the working of his great might which he accomplished in Christ when he raised him from the dead and made him sit at his right hand in the heavenly places, far above all rule and authority and power and dominion, and above every name that is named, not only in this age but also in that which is to come; and he has put all things under his feet and has made him the head over all things for the church, which is his body, the fullness of him who fills all in all.

Reflection

This grandiloquent prayer of Paul at the beginning of his letter, full of phrases rolling one after the other to try and express his rich meaning, is a prayer that we may understand the consequences of the resurrection for ourselves. This is, in fact, the whole theme of the letter, that Christ's being raised to the position of total pre-eminence at God's right hand draws us up too. The measure of God's power in us is his power at work in Christ, and this extends to the whole of creation.

Writing to the Corinthians, Paul had seen all Christians as members of Christ's body, each with his separate and individual function to perform in Christ, and together making up the fullness of Christ. But finally in Ephesians he sees the fullness of Christ as having even greater extension. The exact translation of the last phrase is not at all clear, and it could well mean 'the fullness of him who is totally, in all ways complete'; but the mysterious terms used are such as to convey that there is nothing which lies outside Christ; his influence is all-embracing.

The way in which Paul expresses Christ's relationship to the Church has also developed. In Corinthians all the different members of the body were thought of as together making up Christ; in Ephesians Christ is the head, distinguished from the body which is the Church. But there is a further richness in this; for according to the medical views of the time, the head is not merely the seat of intelligence and so the directing force; from the head comes the nourishment and vigour of the body; it is the mainspring and source of action. He is, then, describing the most vital, continuous and life-giving of all contacts between Christ as head and the Church as body. The power of God is at work in Christ, and the power of Christ is at work in us, the Church.

It is hardly believable that, with this source of strength and life, we can falter. As Paul intended, the knowledge of the pulsating union to Christ, the source of all power, must buoy us up. It is not merely, as often represented, that Christ stands behind us and covers our actions; he supplies the strength in which all our actions are done.

19

THE COMMAND TO EVANGELIZE
THE WORLD

Daniel 7:13-14

I saw in the night visions,
and behold, with the clouds of heaven
    there came one like a son of man,
and he came to the Ancient of Days
    and was presented before him.
And to him was given dominion
    and glory and kingdom,
that all peoples, nations, and languages
    should serve him;
his dominion is an everlasting dominion,
    which shall not pass away,
and his kingdom one
    that shall not be destroyed.

Matthew 28:16-20

Now the eleven disciples went to Galilee, to the mountain
to which Jesus had directed them. And when they saw
him they worshipped him; but some doubted. And Jesus
came and said to them, "All authority in heaven and
on earth has been given to me. Go therefore and make
disciples of all nations, baptizing them in the name of

the Father and of the Son and of the Holy Spirit, teaching them to observe all that I have commanded you; and lo, I am with you always, to the close of the age."

Reflection

The vision of the son of man in the book of Daniel forms the background for Jesus' use of the expression about himself; it suggests the majesty and power of the mysterious figure to whom all sovereignty, glory and kingship are given. Jesus used the title during his earthly life in a way which was typical of his method of self-revelation: with consummate tact he gave the revelation for those who had ears to hear, but at the same time forced no one; he hinted, and left those who willed to reflect, in the light of his words and actions, on the full implications of his claims. Now, in this last meeting of the risen Christ with his disciples, Matthew shows him in a position of commanding majesty on the mountain-top in Galilee, summarizing his commission to the apostles as the Son of Man in his full sovereignty over the universe. It is precisely in this capacity that he sends them out to make disciples of all men.

With this command goes the promise of his ever-present help. The theme of Christ's presence in his Church runs through the gospel of Matthew. At the beginning it is presaged by the name given by the angel 'God with us', as he first comes into the world; and at the end he finally blesses them with the promise to be with them 'to the end of time'. Thus Matthew expresses what is expressed by John in the promise of the presence and guidance of the Spirit. With the charge goes always the promise of the power to fulfil it. And it is no impersonal power; the metaphors which used to be employed to explain grace were faulty in this; for it is nothing like fuel or electricity in virtue of which the machine is enabled to function. Christ's power is not separate from Christ himself, but is his enabling presence, a personal loving presence which means that the Christian acts in his work in the world not merely in virtue of Christ; it is Christ acting through and in the personality of his disciple, not remotely, nor yet destroying the human personality and capacities, but with them, so that it is both we who act and Christ who acts in us.

20

GOD'S WORK OF ART

Romans 7:14-23

We know that the law is spiritual; but I am carnal, sold under sin. I do not understand my own actions. For I do not do what I want, but I do what I do not want, I agree that the law is good. So then it is no longer I that do it, but sin which dwells within me. For I know that nothing good dwells within me, that is, in my flesh. I can will what is right, but I cannot do it. For I do not do the good I want, but the evil I do not want is what I do. Now if I do what I do not want, it is no longer I that do it, but sin which dwells within me.

So I find it to be a law that when I want to do right, evil lies close at hand. For I delight in the law of God, in my inmost self, but I see in my members another law at war with the law of my mind and making me captive to the law of sin which dwells in my members.

Ephesians 2:1-10

And you he made alive, when you were dead through the trespasses and sins in which you once walked, following the course of this world, following the prince of the power of the air, the spirit that is now at work in the sons of disobedience. Among these we all once lived in the passions of our flesh, following the desires of body and mind, and so we were by nature children of wrath, like the rest of mankind. But God, who is rich in mercy, out of the great love with which he loved us, even when we were dead through our trespasses, made us alive together with Christ (by grace you have been saved), and raised us up with him, and made us sit with him in the heavenly places in Christ Jesus, that in the coming ages he might show the immeasurable riches of his grace in kindness towards us in Christ Jesus. For by grace you have been saved through faith; and this is not your own doing, it is the gift of God — not because of works, lest any man should boast. For we are his workmanship, created in Christ Jesus for good works, which God prepared beforehand, that we should walk in them.

Reflection

In this passage of Ephesians Paul is trying to get across the fantastic reversal in our fate and fortunes which has taken place through the resurrection. Christ's place is taken for granted; he is 'far above every Sovereignty, Authority, Power or Domination' or anything else that can be named. But what is so dazzling is the change that has taken place in us. We were dead, lifeless things, helpless in our sins and unable to rise, as the passage from Romans explains in a graphic picture of helplessness; one is reminded of the punch-drunk boxer who cannot stand up, but finds that his limbs simply collapse under him. Life without Christ was no life, because it ended in nothingness and so had fundamentally no purpose; seen aright, this purposelessness pervades even the seeming life and activity which there was. The change which Paul is trying to express bursts the bonds of language, so that he is forced to forge new words: God gave us life in giving it to Christ, in raising Christ he raised us, in enthroning Christ at his right hand he enthroned us: he 'con-enlivened' us, 'con-raised' us, 'con-enthroned' us. It was his very action of exalting Christ which exalted us, not mere accompanying or consequent actions — so real is the union of ourselves to Christ that his history is ours.

The other thought which predominates, as a natural consequence of this, is the undeservedness of our change in position: it is due solely to the unprovoked action of God, a free gift simply because he looked on us with favour. The word for 'grace', twice repeated in this passage, recalls an oriental court where a despot may, unpredictably and without any deserts, grant his favour to anyone he chooses. So with God, his generosity is a totally unprovoked free gift, a pure act of favour based only on his love.

It is the combination of these two elements, the complete change from a state of hopeless death to one of already achieved life, and the total gratuity of this gift, which give us some inkling of our debt — though perhaps even the independent dignity of being a debtor to God is too much for our nothingness.

21

THE ASCENSION

Luke 24:50-53

Then he led them out as far as Bethany, and lifting up his hands he blessed them. While he blessed them he was parted from them and was carried up into heaven. And they worshipped him, and returned to Jerusalem with great joy, and were continually in the temple blessing God.

Acts 1:6-11

So when they had come together, they asked him, "Lord, will you at this time restore the kingdom to Israel?" He said to them, "It is not for you to know times or seasons which the Father has fixed by his own authority. But you shall receive power when the Holy Spirit has come upon you; and you shall be my witness in Jerusalem and in all Judea and Samaria and to the end of the earth." And when he had said this, as they were looking on, he was lifted up and a cloud took him out of their sight. And while they were gazing into heaven as he went, behold, two men stood by them in white robes, and said, "Men of Galilee, why do you stand looking into heaven? This Jesus, who was taken up from you into heaven, will come in the same way as you saw him go into heaven."

Reflection

In these two accounts of the same event by the evangelist Luke the emphasis is slightly different because the viewpoint is different. At the end of the gospel the ascension is a conclusion; at the beginning of the Acts of the Apostles it is an opening.

Thus the keynote of the gospel passage is joy and thanksgiving. Both of these have been prominent throughout the gospel. The angel announced joy to the shepherds at the birth of Christ, as Gabriel had promised Zachary that many people would rejoice in the birth of the precursor; in Luke people seem to be singing, praising God and rejoicing all the time, especially at receiving the message of Christ. It is as though a great joy has broken out on earth with the coming of the Saviour, which is infectious and spreads everywhere. Now at the conclusion of the gospel this joy and thanksgiving provide a quiet cadence which is left resonating and echoing to be also a keynote for the future. The Church is to be full of joy and thanksgiving at the saving work of God in Christ and at the gift of adherence to Christ which has been given to them to complete his work in them.

But in the Acts the glance is wholly forward-looking. With the ascension of Jesus one era is closed and another begins; it is the definitive parting of Christ from his disciples in which he sends them out to carry on his work. They are about to receive the Spirit which will give them power, and then they are to be his witnesses to the ends of the earth. They are not to remain staring, star-struck, into heaven, nor are they to indulge in dreams about the restoration of Israel; it is for them to work until he comes at the time which only the Father knows. The world is open and the promise of help is here.

The final scene, then, of Christ's life on earth, both in Matthew and in Luke, is limitlessly open on the future. The risen Christ entrusts his Church to men; they are to administer it for him, though always in the power of his final blessing. In one way he can be said to part with the words 'It is up to you now'; in another way one must be sure that the strength is all his.

22

THE RACE FOR THE FINISH

Philippians 1:20-24

It is my eager expectation and hope that I shall not be at all ashamed, but that with full courage now as always Christ will be honoured in my body, whether by life or by death. For to me to live is Christ, and to die is gain. If it is to be life in the flesh, that means fruitful labour for me. Yet which I shall choose I cannot tell. I am hard pressed between the two. My desire is to depart and be with Christ, for that is far better. But to remain in the flesh is more necessary on your account.

Philippians 3:7-14

But whatever gain I had, I counted as loss for the sake of Christ. Indeed I count everything as loss because of the surpassing worth of knowing Christ Jesus my Lord. For his sake I have suffered the loss of all things, and count them as refuse, in order that I may gain Christ and be found in him, not having a righteousness of my own, based on law, but that which is through faith in Christ, the righteousness from God that depends on faith; that I may know him and the power of his resurrection, and may share his sufferings, becoming like him in his death, that if possible I may attain the resurrection from the dead.

Not that I have already obtained this or am already perfect; but I press on to make it my own, because Christ Jesus has made me his own. Brethren, I do not consider that I have made it my own; but one thing I do, forgetting what lies behind and straining forward to what lies ahead, I press on toward the goal for the prize of the upward call of God in Christ Jesus.

Reflection

It seems that Paul is ageing, or at least tiring, when he comes to write to the Philippians like this; he is already straining towards the finish. But, as he sees in the first passage, life or death makes little difference to him; for life is already Christ; it is only that death would be more, the point which brings completion and blossoming of the seed which is already there. The extent to which Paul lives this truth about Christ in him appears from the second passage: formerly as a Pharisee his one desire had been to fulfil the law and win justification before God by his punctilious observance; it was the law, circumcision, his Hebrew ancestry which were all his pride. But now all these elements of his life before he was seized by Christ count as nothing; they really belong to a life that is past, belonging as though to another person; when Paul says we have been born again by baptism he really means that it is a new life, in the power of the resurrection; the only thing that matters is to conform as closely as possible to the pattern of Christ and imitate the model of Christ in every respect. Hence Paul's longing even for suffering if it will fill up the measure of the sufferings of Christ.

It is easy enough to say in the abstract that we want to share the life of Christ. We become less enthusiastic when it comes to sharing the sufferings of Christ. The reality that we have cast aside our old lives and selves is not so total as it was for Paul. We have other objects in view, among them being to avoid too much unnecessary suffering; we do not pursue the logic which is his, that if we share his life we are positively eager to press on to the goal of full assimilation to him in suffering and death, that even the seeming separation from him of life in this world and this body is a positive disadvantage; at the finishing-line we collapse into him.

23

THE LAMB THAT WAS SLAIN

Revelation 5:1-14

And I saw in the right hand of him who was seated on the throne a scroll written within and on the back, sealed with seven seals; and I saw a strong angel proclaiming with a loud voice, "Who is worthy to open the scroll and break its seals?" And no one in heaven or on earth or under the earth was able to open the scroll or to look into it, and I wept much that no one was found worthy to open the scroll or to look into it. Then one of the elders said to me, "Weep not; lo, the Lion of the tribe of Judah, the Root of David, has conquered, so that he can open the scroll and its seven seals."

And between the throne and the four living creatures and among the elders, I saw a Lamb standing, as though it had been slain, with seven horns and with seven eyes, which are the seven spirits of God sent out into all the earth; and he went and took the scroll from the right hand of him who was seated on the throne. And when he had taken the scroll, the four living creatures and the twenty-four elders fell down before the Lamb, each holding a harp, and with golden bowls full of incense, which are the prayers of the saints; and they sang a new song saying,

"Worthy are thou to take the scroll
and open its seals,

for thou wast slain and by thy blood
  didst ransom men for God
from every tribe and tongue and people
  and nation,
and hast made them a kingdom and
  priests to our God,
and they shall reign on earth."

Then I looked, and I heard around the throne and the living creatures and the elders the voice of many angels, numbering myriads of myriads and thousands of thousands, saying with a loud voice, "Worthy is the Lamb who was slain, to receive power and wealth and wisdom and might and honour and glory and blessing!" And I heard every creature in heaven and on earth and under the earth and in the sea, and all therein, saying, "To him who sits upon the throne and to the Lamb be blessing and honour and glory and might for ever and ever!" And the four living creatures said, "Amen!" and the elders fell down and worshipped.

Reflection

The book of Revelation has such riches of symbolism and imagery that a deep biblical culture is needed for the details to be appreciated; but at the same time no explanation is necessary or adequate to convey the impression of splendour which it gives. The chief purpose of the book is to comfort Christians under persecution with the knowledge of eventual deliverance. Here it is expressed by the triumph of the Lamb, who had himself been sacrificed and is now granted sovereignty. The scroll which he takes contains the secrets of history, and more especially the secrets of the final history when God's triumph will be made manifest; he is, then, the Lord of history and controls its unfolding. Thus everything in heaven and on earth pays homage to him, not only men but angels, the powers of heaven and every living creature on earth. And always in mind is the fact that it is because he has been sacrificed that he attains this position. His suffering and the agony and fear of death are not an end but are no more than a passage to glory. So for those who follow him, too, persecution is but a means to an end, that they may reign with him as they have joined him in his suffering.

The conception of the Lamb as Lord of history seems paradoxical: how can Christ be Lord of the history which is so full of disasters and suffering, and especially of war and injustice perpetrated in his name? As with the individual tragedies of sickness and bereavement which we meet from day to day, so with the larger canvas of history as a whole, we cannot hope to judge how Christ is directing them. Sometimes it becomes clear how the apparently hopeless tragedy has in fact brought greater depth and even eventual happiness, how the betrayal has led to a richer renewal. But more often it remains inscrutable. It is in these cases that we must fall back on the vision of the book of Revelation in the dim but certain light of faith, and in confidence in the triumph of the Lamb that was slain.

24

THE HEAVENLY JERUSALEM

Ezekiel 40:1-4

In the twenty-fifth year of our exile, at the beginning of the year, on the tenth day of the month, in the fourteenth year after the city was conquered, on that very day, the hand of the Lord was upon me, and brought me in the visions of God into the land of Israel, and set me down upon a very high mountain, on which was a structure like a city opposite me. When he brought me there, behold, there was a man, whose appearance was like bronze, with a line of flax and a measuring reed in his hand; and he was standing in the gateway. And the man said to me, "Son of man, look with your eyes, and hear with your ears, and set your mind upon all that I shall show you, for you were brought here in order that I might show it to you; declare all that you see to the house of Israel."

Revelation 21:9-14, 22:1-5

Then came one of the seven angels who had the seven bowls full of the seven last plagues, and spoke to me, saying, "Come, I will show you the Bride, the wife of the Lamb." And in the Spirit he carried me away to a great, high mountain, and showed me the holy city Jerusalem coming down out of heaven from God, having the glory of God, its radiance like a most rare jewel, like a jasper, clear as crystal. It had a great, high wall, with twelve gates, and at the gates twelve angels, and on the gates the names of the twelve tribes of the sons of Israel were inscribed; on the east three gates, on the north three gates, on the south three gates, and on the west three gates. And the wall of the city had twelve foundations, and on them the twelve names of the twelve apostles of the Lamb.

Then he showed me the river of the water of life, bright as crystal, flowing from the throne of God and of the Lamb through the middle of the street of the city; also, on either side of the river, the tree of life with its twelve kinds of fruit, yielding its fruit each month; and the leaves of the tree were for the healing of the nations. There shall no more be anything accursed, but the throne of God and of the Lamb shall be in it, and his servants shall worship him; they shall see his face, and his name shall be on their foreheads. And night shall be no more; they need no light of lamp or sun, for the Lord God will be their light, and they shall reign for ever and ever.

Reflection

During the exile of the chosen people in Babylon, at what seemed the most hopeless moment of their history, Ezekiel reassured them by a minute description of the new Jerusalem which the messiah would establish. The book of Revelation uses the same device to give the persecuted Christian a vision of the goal to which his pilgrimage leads. The two most striking features about it are the Lamb who is its centre and its temple, and the river of life. The water of life has a vivid significance in the dry land of Palestine, so close to the desert, where any stream is truly a source of life. In John's gospel Jesus is frequently pointed out as the source of life, and under the same metaphor of water with his promise 'If anyone thirst, let him come to me and drink . . . out of his heart shall flow rivers of living water' (John 7: 37-38). Living water conjures up the ideas of life and fruitfulness, and so of plenty, in fact of everything which brings joy to life and liberates it from barren monotony; it suggests also relief from burning heat and toil, and yet with its continuous flow it suggests an active repose, full of vigour and gentle purpose. So it is a perfect symbol of the new life which Christ came to bring, so that believing we might have life through his name (John 20: 31). And it is not merely earthly life, but a life which endures for eternity. Such is the river of life which flows out from under the throne and flows through the centre of the city, at which all the inhabitants of the city may drink.

The other dominant feature of this new Jerusalem is the aura of light which surrounds and pervades everywhere. Nowhere is there darkness or gloom of sorrow or shame, but all is bathed in clear light. The glory of God is always pictured in the Old Testament under the image of brightness, dazzling and powerful, able to purify as well as illumine, a fierce light which can burn as well as warm, according to the dispositions of those who receive it. But here in the peace of the holy city it is uniquely beneficent, a golden light in which sparkles the brilliance of the precious stones which form the gates. The source of this light, as of the living water, is the Lord God and the Lamb. As they together form the temple which is the centre of the city, and share the throne, so they are together its light and radiance.

The Lamb who was slain and yet lives is then the centre of the city; the risen Christ is seen as the centre of saved creation. Nor is this to occur only at the end of time; the city exists already, and in it the Lamb already gives light and life.

25

THE FINAL CONSUMMATION

Romans 5:14-18

Adam was a type of the one who was to come. But the free gift is not like the trespass. For if many died through one man's trespass much more have the grace of God and the free gift in the grace of that one man Jesus Christ abounded for many. And the free gift is not like the effect of that one man's sin. For the judgment following one trespass brought condemnation, but the free gift following many trespasses brings justification. If, because of one man's trespass, death reigned through that one man, much more will those who receive the abundance of grace and the free gift of righteousness reign in life through the one man Jesus Christ.

Then as one man's trespass led to condemnation for all men, so one man's act of righteousness leads to acquittal and life for all men.

1 Corinthians 15:20-28

But in fact Christ has been raised from the dead, the first fruits of those who have fallen asleep. For as by a man came death, by a man has come also the resurrection of the dead. For as in Adam all die, so also in Christ shall all be made alive. But each in his own order: Christ the first fruits, then at his coming those who belong to Christ. Then comes the end, when he delivers the kingdom to God the Father after destroying every rule and every authority and power. For he must reign until he has put all his enemies under his feet. The last enemy to be destroyed is death. For God has put all things in subjection under his feet. But when it says, "All things are put in subjection under him," it is plain that he is excepted who put all things under him. When all things are subjected to him, then the Son himself will also be subjected to him who put all things under him, that God may be everything to everyone.

Reflection

The state in which we now are is determined by the second Adam. Adam, meaning 'Man', is the name given to the theoretical founder of the human race who — whatever the solution to the problems about whether such a man, from whom all men are sprung, existed or not — represents all mankind. 'In Adam all men fell and died' is a statement primarily about the present natural state of man alienated from God and with a hopeless future. When Paul teaches that Adam prefigured Christ we may understand that as Adam is represented as the founder of humanity, Christ is the re-founder; further, the one who prefigures has meaning only in function of the one he prefigures: humanity has meaning only in so far as it looks to Christ; in him it reaches its culminating point, the goal to which it had tended from the first. There was no life before Christ brought life to humanity by his obedience.

The life brought by Christ began in and through obedience to God, as death had been through disobedience. It is not a transitory act of obedience, but the life consists in a permanent state of obedience, a relationship to God of submission. This is no external demand of God, after the model of a domineering master who exacts obedience, but the life-condition of man is this true relationship to God which gives him the dependence on and attachment to God without which he cannot live.

As we know all too well from experience of ourselves, by baptism and adherence to Christ perfect obedience and so full life are not immediately attained. Transformation of the individual into Christ is a gradual process, and the same is true of humanity. All men will be brought to life in Christ but not immediately. But the final picture is that of Christ as the first-fruit of living humanity and its natural king, who has received from God the power over the whole universe promised to the Son of Man of Daniel's vision, presenting the redeemed and living world to his Father. Christ is the Omega point of Teilhard de Chardin, the point which is the culmination of evolution, the keystone which makes sense of it all. When he presents redeemed humanity to the Father then God is all in all.

BIBLE PASSAGES USED

OLD TESTAMENT

NEW TESTAMENT